MEL BAY PRESENTS

MW00387927

Classics
FOR UKULELE

by Ondřej Šárek

1 2 3 4 5 6 7 8 9 0

Visit us on the Web at www.melbay.com — E-mail us at email@melbay.com

Contents

Introduction

Many greetings to all ukulele players. Perhaps some consider a ukulele to be just a marginal instrument that accompanies singing. This is not the case. These dots that you hold in your hands are illustrations which will allow you to play solo melodies plus classical music on the ukulele. Now you can show your friends – symphonic orchestra players that it is possible to play these wonderful pieces on the ukulele.

The style of music presented here range from the Renaissance to the Romantic periods by renowned composers—providing several quality tunes to choose from.

Here are a few performance notes:

Pieces are written for the uke tuned in the key of C (G4-C4-E4-A4). However, you do not have to play all the pieces on the instrument tuned to "C." Play the *First Movement* from "Symphony No. 5" by Beethoven in D (A4-D4-F#4-B4). You will regain the original key and be able to play it with orchestral record.

I have used this notation. The G string is noted an octave lower than sounds. It is a less common notation. I chose it because the voices are more "arranged" and do not cross the dots. It allows you to better recognize which string you are to play.

Certainly, some of the pieces would be possible to play by a plectrum like "Song to the Moon" by Dvorák, but that would not be the same as the original. The pieces are arranged for finger picking. Mostly, by a thumb, an index finger and a middle finger of the right hand. On the other hand, the ring finger is better to use as in *Ave Maria* by Bach-Gounod.

I wish you much success and enjoyment in the practice and performance of these timeless pieces.

Ondrej Sarek

Angelica Bilta

Francesco Landini
arr: Ondrej Sarek

Moderato

Fine

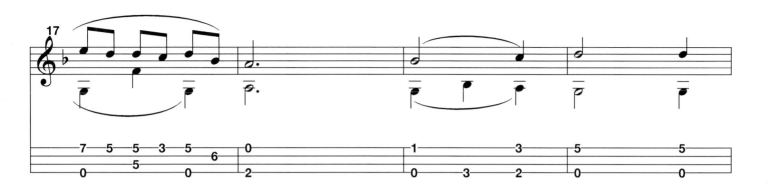

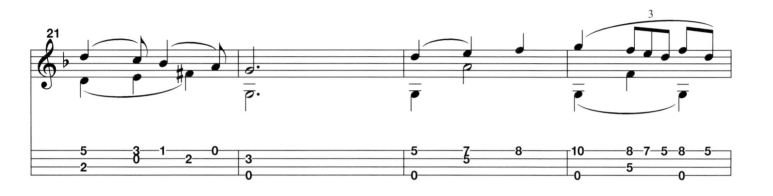

D.C. al Fine

Lasciatemi Morire

from opera "L'Arianna"

Claudio Monteverdi
arr: Ondrej Sarek

Musette

from "The Notebook of Anna Magdalena Bach"

Johann Sebastian Bach
arr: Ondrej Sarek

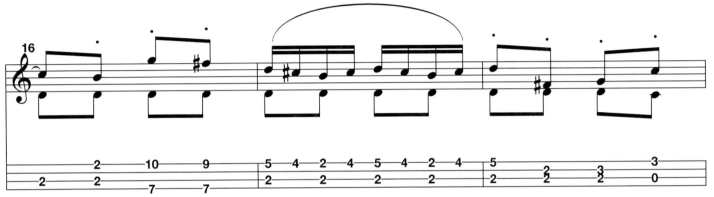

D.C. al Fine

Menuet

Georg Friedrich Händel
arr: Ondrej Sarek

Andantino

Ave Verum Corpus

Wolfgang Amadeus Mozart
arr: Ondrej Sarek

Adagio

14

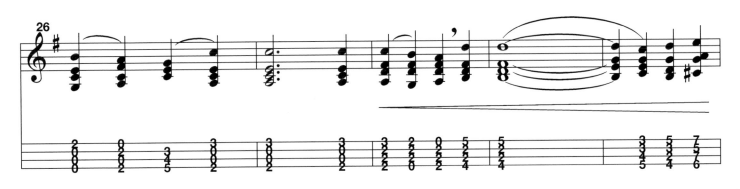

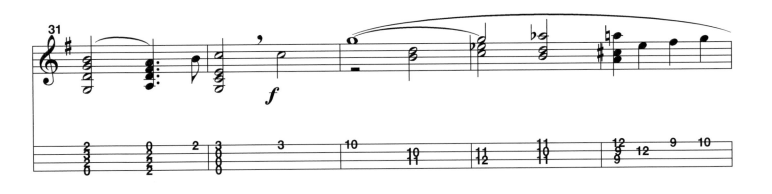

Sonata

Opus KV 331

Wolfgang Amadeus Mozart
arr: Ondrej Sarek

Andante grazioso

This page has been left blank to avoid awkward page turns.

Moonlight Sonata

Op. 27 No. 2

Ludwig van Beethoven
arr: Ondrej Sarek

Adagio

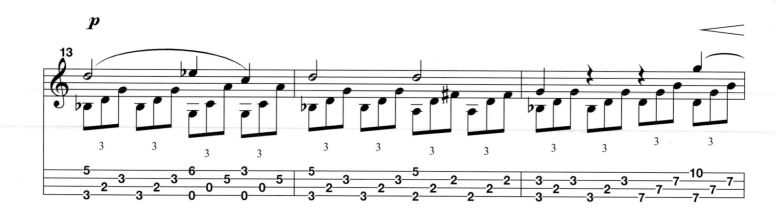

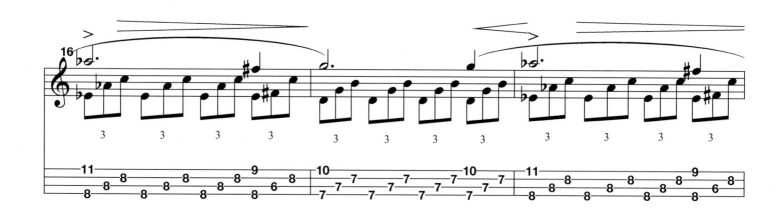

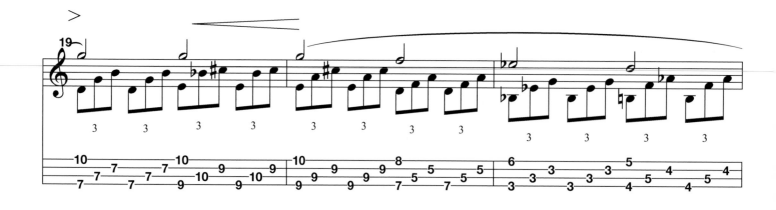

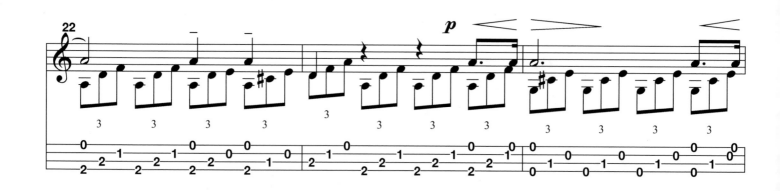

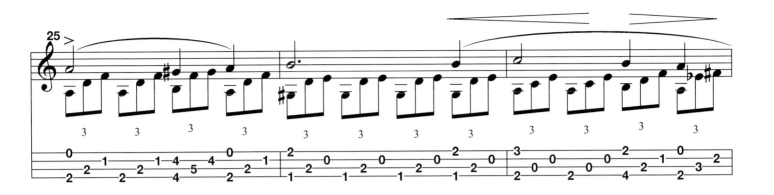

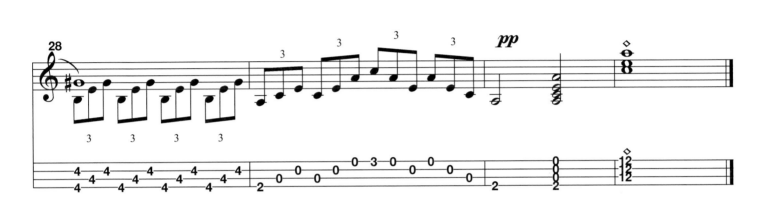

First Movement

from "Symphony No. 5"

Ludwig van Beethoven
arr: Ondrej Sarek

Allegro con brio

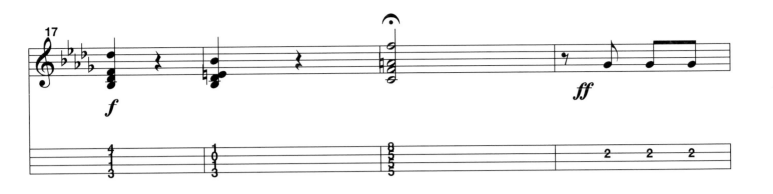

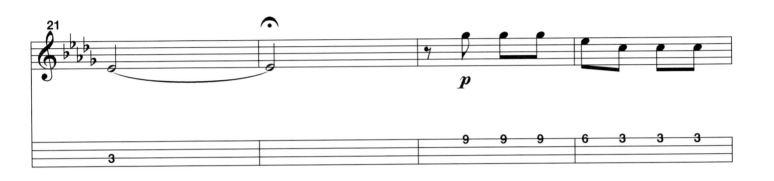

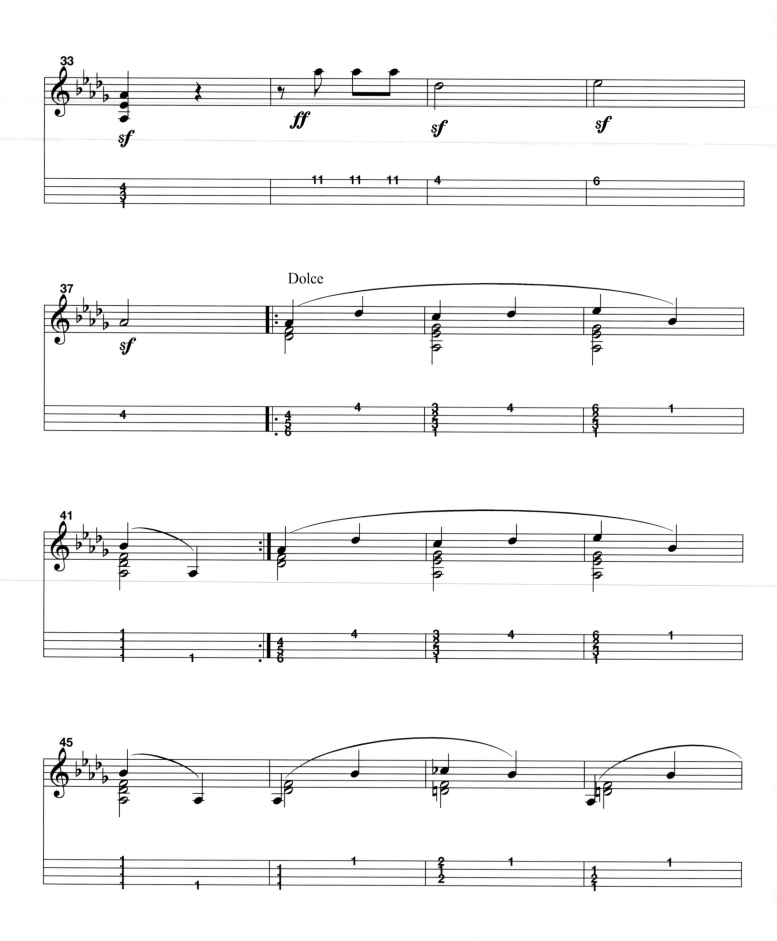

Ave Maria

Johann Sebastian Bach/
Charles Francois Gounod
arr: Ondrej Sarek

Moderato

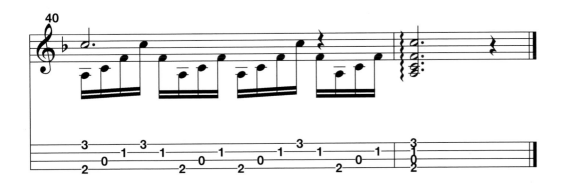

Hungarian Dance No. 5

Johannes Brahms
arr: Ondrej Sarek

Allegro

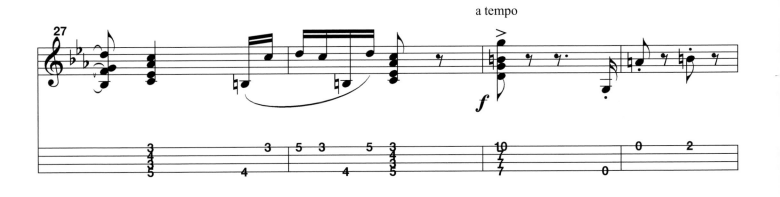

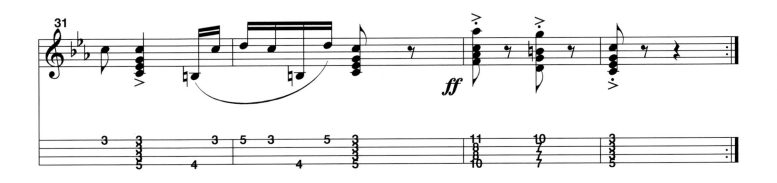

Waltz

from ballet "Swan Lake"

Pyotr Ilyich Tchaikovsky
arr: Ondrej Sarek

Waltz

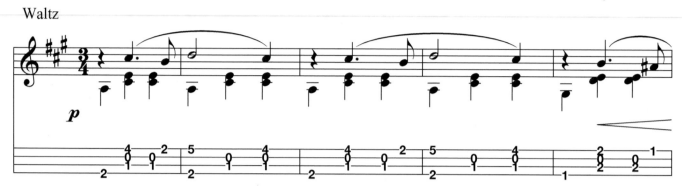

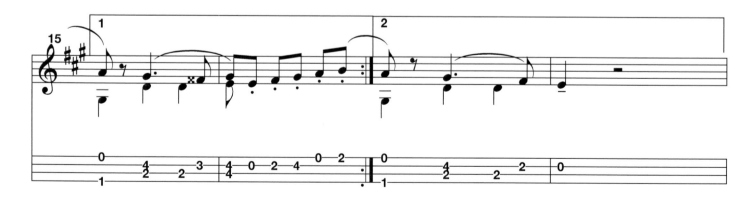

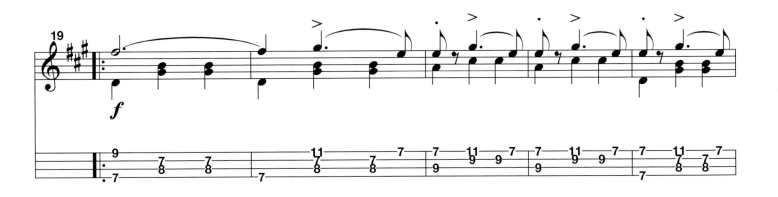

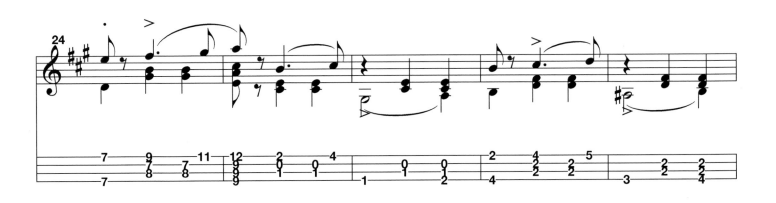

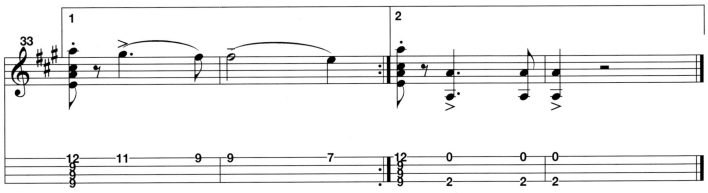

Old French Song

from "Album for the Young"

Pyotr Ilyich Tchaikovsky
arr: Ondrej Sarek

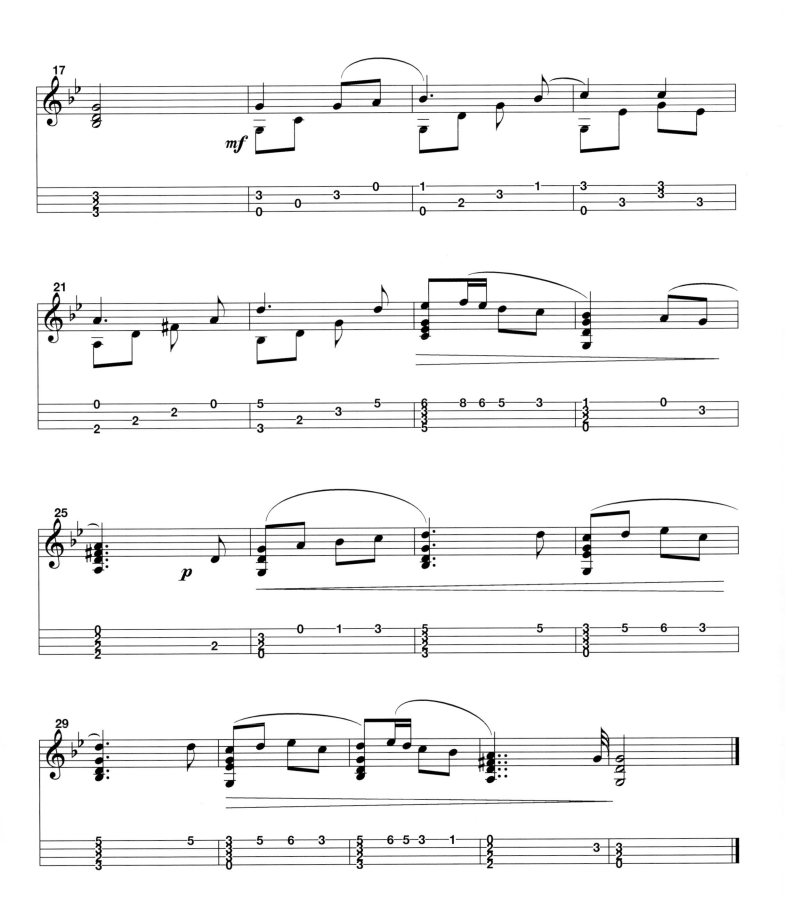

Toreador Song

from opera "Carmen"

Georges Bizet
arr: Ondrej Sarek

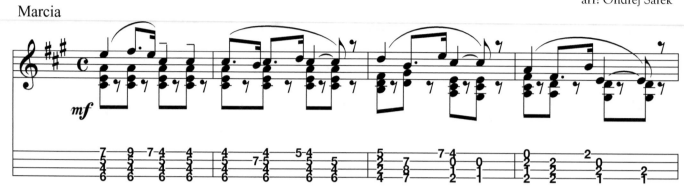

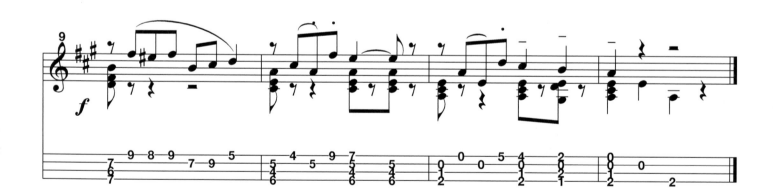

Ride of the Valkyries

from opera "Die Walküre"

Richard Wagner
arr: Ondrej Sarek

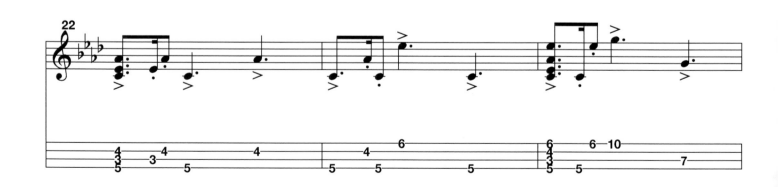

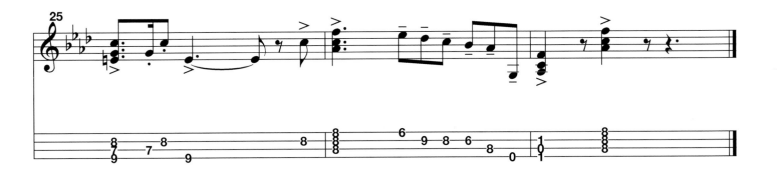

Wiegenlied

Op. 98 No. 2

Franz Schubert
arr: Ondrej Sarek

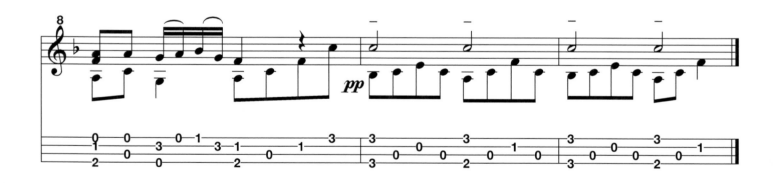

Wedding March

from "A Midsummer Night's Dream"

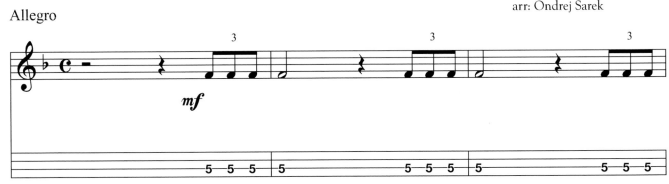

Felix Mendelssohn-Bartholdy
arr: Ondrej Sarek

Allegro

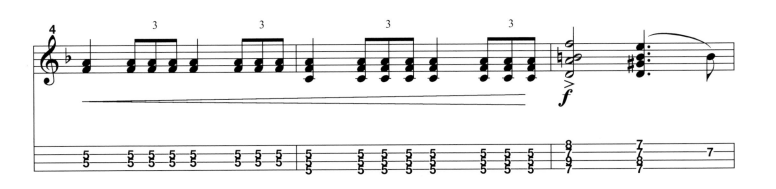

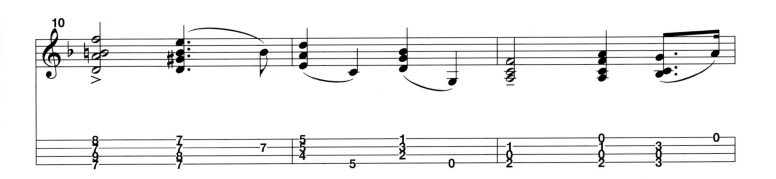

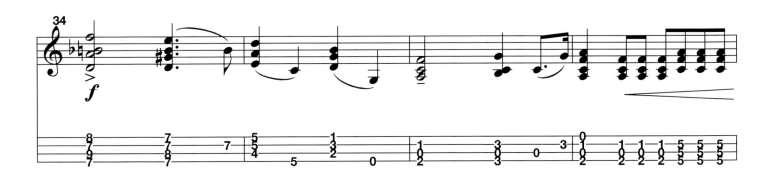

To Wander

from song cycle "Die schöne Müllerin"

Franz Schubert
arr: Ondrej Sarek

Allegro moderato

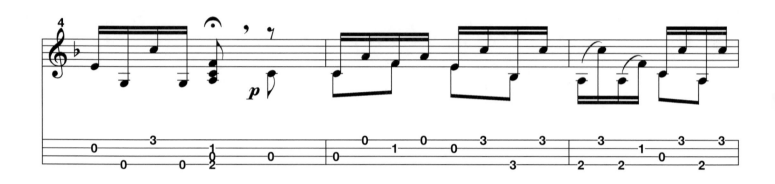

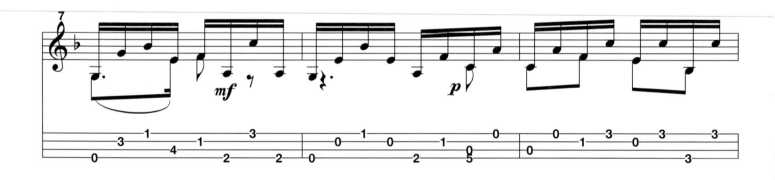

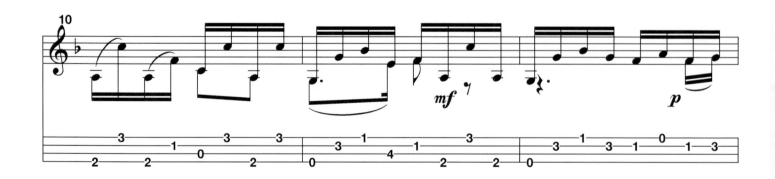

God Is My Shepherd

from song cycle "Biblical Songs"

Antonín Dvořák
arr: Ondrej Sarek

Andante

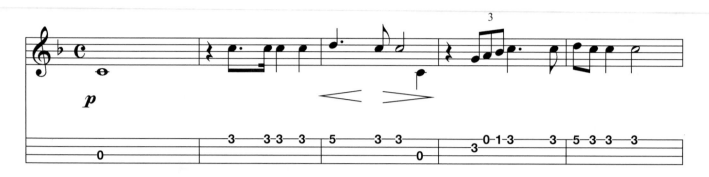

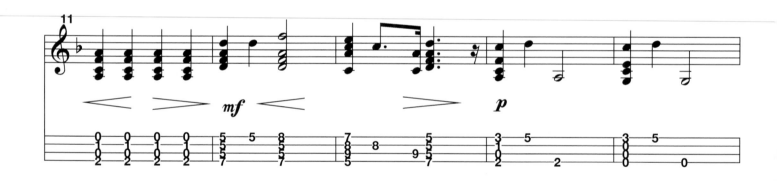

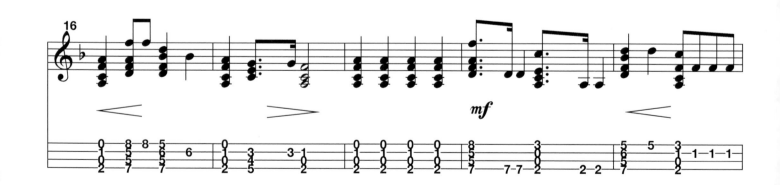

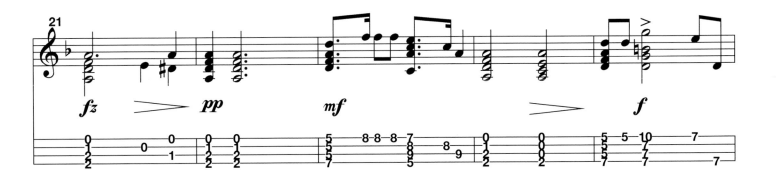

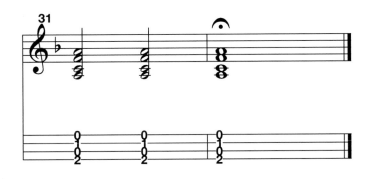

Solveig's Song

from "Peer Gynt"

Edvard Grieg
arr: Ondrej Sarek

Andante

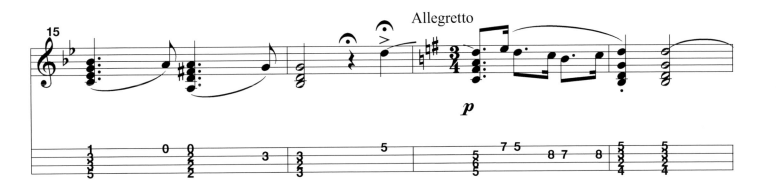

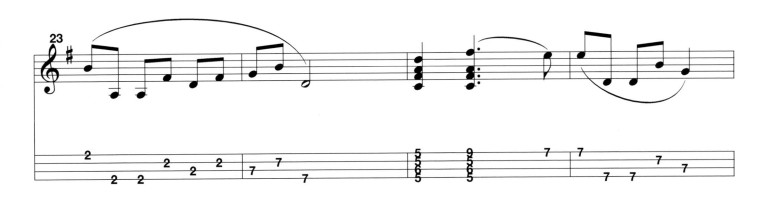

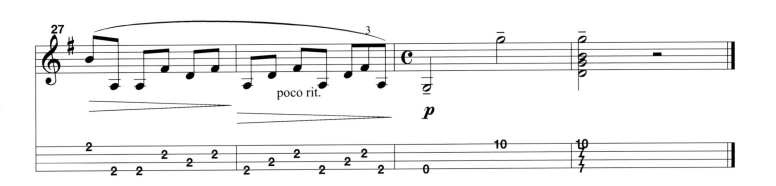

Song to the Moon

from opera "Rusalka"

Antonín Dvořák
arr: Ondrej Sarek

Larghetto

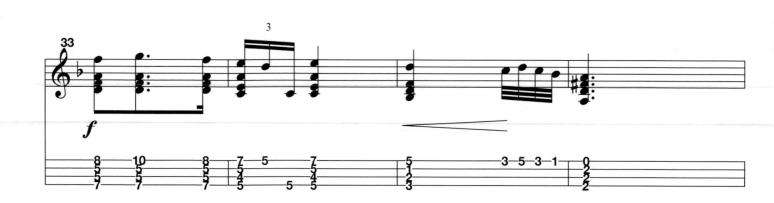

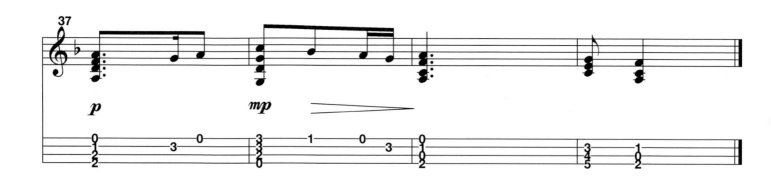